Helping Children See Jesus

ISBN: 978-1-64104-018-1

CONVERSION
New Testament Volume 17: Acts Part 4

Author: Ruth B. Greiner
Illustrator: Frances H. Hertzler
Colorization courtesy of Good Life Ministries
Typesetting and Layout: Morgan Melton, Patricia Pope

© 2018 Bible Visuals International
PO Box 153, Akron, PA 17501-0153
Phone: (717) 859-1131
www.biblevisuals.org

All rights reserved. No part of this publication may be reproduced, stored in a retrieval system or transmitted in any form by any means, electronic, mechanical, photocopy, recording or otherwise, without the prior permission of the publisher, except as provided by USA copyright law.

RELATED ITEMS

To access related items (such as activities, memory verse posters and translated texts) please visit our web store at shop.biblevisuals.org and enter 1017 in the search box on the page.

FREE TEXT DOWNLOAD

To access a FREE printable copy of the teaching text (PDF format) in English or other available languages, enter S1017DL in the search box. Add the item to your cart, and use coupon code XTACSV17 at checkout. Once your order is processed you will receive an email with a link to the free download.

CONVERSION is turning *to* God and His new life in Christ and turning away *from* sin and the old life.

When Paul turned *to* Christ, he turned *from* hating the Lord. He had an about face so that after his conversion, instead of opposing the Gospel, he loved it and loved to preach it.

Except ye be converted, and become as little children, ye shall not enter into the kingdom of Heaven.

Matthew 18:3b

Lesson 1
SAUL–A JEW IS CONVERTED

NOTE TO THE TEACHER

Conversion is a complete turning about–turning to God from sin. It is a change which affects heart and life in every area. (Use the outside back cover to illustrate conversion.)

No one is born a Christian. Nor can anyone be educated into Christianity. One cannot be made a Christian by baptism or any religious ceremony. To become a Christian and be assured of eternal life in Heaven, a person must be genuinely converted–completely turned about.

Every unconverted soul is a sinner in the kingdom of darkness, under the power of Satan and on the way to hell. (See John 3:18-19; Acts 26:18; Ephesians 5:8; Colossians 1:13; 1 Peter 2:9.) When that individual turns to Jesus Christ and receives Him as Lord and Saviour, he is no longer in Satan's kingdom of darkness. Instead he belongs to the kingdom of God's dear Son.

Saul was converted on his way to Damascus. When the light from Heaven shone on him and the voice spoke to him, immediately he cried, "Who are You, Lord?" And, a moment later, "Lord, what do You want me to do?" No one "can say that Jesus is the Lord, but by the Holy Spirit" (1 Corinthians 12:3). Since Saul used the name "Lord" on the Damascus road, we believe he accepted Christ Jesus the Lord at that time. (See also Romans 10:9-10.)

When Saul responded to the voice of Jesus, it was as if he said, "Lord, from now on I am Yours. I belong to You. You are my Lord. What do You want me to do?" From the moment of his conversion he was ready to yield himself wholly to the One who died to redeem him. He was completely turned about.

A map appears on pages 16 and 17. We have included the places named in these lessons. You may wish to add the names of other areas Paul visited during his early ministry. (See Acts 13-16.) The map will help your students to appreciate the extent of Paul's efforts. (In volume 17, *Service*, we shall continue to study Paul's missionary journeys.)

Encourage your students to point on the map to the places as they are named in the lesson.

Scripture to be studied: Acts 8:1-3; 9:1-22; 22:1-16; 26:4-20

The *aim* of the lesson: To show that at Saul's conversion he turned about completely and served the Lord.

What your students should *know*: One must turn to God–be converted–to have the joy of sins forgiven.

What your students should *feel*: A desire to have their sins forgiven.

What your students should *do*: Believe in the Lord Jesus Christ as the Son of God and receive Him as Saviour.

Lesson outline (for the teacher's and students' notebooks):
1. Saul imprisons the Christians (Acts 8:1-3; 22:1-4; 26:4-11).
2. Saul hunts the Christians to capture them (Acts 9:1-2; 22:5; 26:11-12).
3. The Lord speaks to Saul (Acts 9:3-19; 22:6-16; 26:13-18).
4. Saul preaches about Jesus (Acts 9:20-22; 26:19-20).

The verse to be memorized:

Except ye be converted, and become as little children, ye shall not enter into the kingdom of Heaven. (Matthew 18:3)

THE LESSON

Saul was a proud man who had been born in Tarsus (the capital city of Cilicia). As a boy he had learned the Greek language and the customs of the Greek people. But his Hebrew parents wanted him also to have a good Jewish education. So they sent Saul to Jerusalem to be taught by Gamaliel, a wise teacher. Saul listened carefully to the instructions of this much respected doctor of religious law. He learned the Jewish laws, obeyed them and became a strict Pharisee. Saul believed, as did the other Pharisees, that the way to Heaven was earned by obeying the Jewish laws.

At this time Saul also became acquainted with some Christians. But he did not agree with them. Indeed, he despised them! Saul had never seen the Lord Jesus, but he had learned much about Him. He knew that the Christians referred to Him as the Son of God. Saul had heard of Christ's crucifixion. He doubtless thought to himself, *Jesus is dead. Why, then, do His followers keep on teaching about Him?* When Saul heard the Apostle Stephen preaching about Jesus, he agreed that Stephen should be killed. So when Stephen was stoned, Saul guarded the coats of the men who hurled the stones.

1. SAUL IMPRISONS THE CHRISTIANS
Acts 8:1-3; 22:1-4; 26:4-11

Saul was certain he was doing right. He thought it pleased God when Christians were killed. He was not satisfied to see only one man die–he wanted all Christians destroyed!

Show Illustration #1

So he went from house to house and dragged the Christians–both men and women–to prison.

The Christians were willing to suffer and, if need be, to die for Christ's sake. But they wanted other people to know about the Lord Jesus. Many of them, therefore, escaped from Jerusalem and fled to other cities. There they did what the Lord had earlier commanded–that is, they told the Gospel and urged their listeners to place their trust in the Lord and receive Him as Saviour.

2. SAUL HUNTS THE CHRISTIANS TO CAPTURE THEM
Acts 9:1-2; 22:5; 26:11-12

Do you suppose Saul stopped hunting the Christians who fled? No, indeed! He hurried to the high priest in Jerusalem and told him of the Christians who had escaped–some going as far as Damascus (a city about 240 kilometers from Jerusalem).

Show Illustration #2

"I want to go to Damascus," Saul told the high priest, "to capture the men and women who are following the Way of Jesus. I shall bring them back here to Jerusalem. But I need men to go with me. And I must have a letter of permission written and signed by you, addressed to the leaders of the Jews in Damascus."

The high priest gave him the letter. Soon Saul was on his way, taking a police force with him.

3. THE LORD SPEAKS TO SAUL
Acts 9:3-19; 22:6-16; 26:13-18

He was almost to Damascus when suddenly a light, brighter than the noon sun, shined upon Saul and his men. They were so afraid that they fell to the ground. All heard a voice, but Saul alone understood the voice which said, "Saul, Saul, why are you persecuting Me?"

Saul answered, "Who are You, Lord?"

"I am Jesus whom you are persecuting," came the answer. Saul was actually hearing the voice of the Lord Jesus Christ, the One whom he thought to be dead. Until this time Saul believed he had been persecuting *Christians*. But according to what he now heard, it was *Jesus* whom he had been persecuting. And since this voice was coming to him from Heaven, he realized that Jesus is truly the Son of God.

Immediately Saul cried, "Lord, what do You want me to do?"

"Get up and go into the city and you will be told what you must do," the Lord answered.

Saul got up and looked about. But he could not see his men. He could not see the road. He could not see the trees or sky. He was blind–blinded by the glory of the light that had shined from the Saviour's face.

Show Illustration #3

Saul's men took him by the hand and led him into the city of Damascus, to the house of a man named Judas. One day . . . two days . . . three days Saul groped about the house in blindness. He did not eat or drink. He thought of the Lord continually and prayed as he had never prayed before.

In another part of the city lived a follower of Jesus named Ananias. He was a godly man and well thought of by the Jews who lived nearby.

To him the Lord appeared in a vision and said, "Ananias." Ananias answered, "I am here, Lord."

"Get up," the Lord said. "Go to the house of Judas on Straight Street. Ask to see Saul of Tarsus. He is praying right now."

Ananias wondered, *How can anyone as cruel as Saul be praying?* To the Lord he said, "Many people tell about this man and the evil he has done to Your followers in Jerusalem. I have also heard that he now has permission from the chief priests to take all Christians here as prisoners."

"Go to Saul," the Lord answered, "for I have chosen to use him in a special way. He will speak of Me to the Gentiles (people who are not Jews), and to kings, and to the Jews. And I shall show him that he will suffer greatly for My sake."

Ananias went to Straight Street. When he found Saul, he placed his hands on him, saying, "Brother Saul, the Lord Jesus who appeared to you has sent me that you might receive your sight and be filled with the Holy Spirit."

Immediately Saul's eyes were opened. He could see! He was baptized at once, so others knew he was indeed a true believer in the Lord Jesus.

Then he ate a good meal and was strengthened. Saul was a new man. He had been converted. He was completely turned about. He became a new person in Christ. (See 2 Corinthians 5:17.) He knew it. Ananias knew it. Saul no longer hated the Lord Jesus; he loved Him. He acknowledged Him as the Son of God. Instead of hating Christians, he loved them. He wanted to tell them of the wonderful change that was his. He could not keep his conversion a secret.

4. SAUL PREACHES ABOUT JESUS
Acts 9:20-22; 26:19-20

Show Illustration #4

He went into the synagogues in Damascus and told everyone the good news about Jesus, the Son of God.

All who heard him were amazed. They asked, "Is this the man who persecuted and destroyed the followers of Jesus in Jerusalem? Is he the one who came to capture the Christians?"

Yes, this was the same man. But now he was converted. He had been changed completely by God's Holy Spirit.

Saul was educated, wealthy and had tried to please God. But in order to get to Heaven he had to be converted. He had to turn to God, truly believing in His Son, the Lord Jesus Christ, receiving Him as Saviour. Only then could he know the joy of having his sins forgiven; only then could he really please and serve God.

Have you been converted? Has there been a time in your life when you have been "turned about" and changed completely into a new person in Christ? Matthew 18:3 says that unless you are converted, you will not enter the kingdom of Heaven.

Lesson 2
CORNELIUS–A GENTILE–IS CONVERTED

NOTE TO THE TEACHER

Acts 1—9 record the Gospel witness of Peter and the other apostles to *Jews* in Jerusalem, Judea, Samaria and Galilee. But our Lord commanded them to go to the uttermost parts of the earth and preach the Gospel to *all* people.

It was months and years, however, before they obeyed the last part of the command. There is no record of any apostle going to the Gentiles until one of the Gentiles (Cornelius) actually sent for Peter and asked him to come!

Cornelius was prepared by God Himself to hear the Gospel. It is no surprise, therefore, that he gladly received the truth as soon as he heard it from Peter.

Peter, the Gospel messenger, also had to be prepared by God. Peter was prejudiced against Gentiles. For hundreds of years God had dealt directly only with His specially chosen people, the Jews. Peter believed it would always be the same. But in a remarkable way, God showed Peter that there was no longer any difference between Jews and Gentiles. All are sinners before God; all have to be saved.

To Peter's credit, once he understood the truth of God, immediately obeyed and went right into the home of Cornelius (an unthinkable thing for a Jew to do) and preached to him.

Depending upon the age, understanding and background of your students, you may want to stress the following truth: Cornelius, a commanding officer of the Roman Army, bowed down reverently before Peter–a poor, converted Jewish fisherman. Peter did not put out his hand saying, "You may kiss the ring on my finger." He said, "Stand up; I myself also am a man."

Scripture to be studied: Acts 10:1-48; 11:1-18

The *aim* of the lesson: To show how the Gospel was first given to the Gentiles.

What your students should *know*: Until a person trusts in the Lord Jesus Christ as Saviour, he does not have a right relationship with God.

What your students should *feel*: A desire to have a right relationship with God.

What your students should *do*: Believe in the Lord Jesus as the Son of God and turn to Him as Saviour.

Lesson outline (for the teacher's and students' notebooks):

1. Peter, a Jew, has a vision (Acts 10:1-16; 11:1-10).
2. Peter has Gentile visitors (Acts 10:17-22; 11:11).
3. Peter goes to the house of Cornelius, a Gentile (Acts 10:23-35; 11:12-14).
4. Peter preaches the Gospel to Cornelius (Acts 10:36-48; 11:15-18).

The verse to be memorized:

Except ye be converted, and become as little children, ye shall not enter into the kingdom of Heaven. (Matthew 18:3)

THE LESSON

"Capture the Christians!" "Throw them into prison!" "Put them to death!" These were the commands of the enemies of the first Christians. These enemies were angry at those who dared to preach that Jesus is the Son of God.

But their threats and cruel tortures did not stop the Christians from spreading the news about Jesus Christ. Nothing kept them from telling that Jesus died for the sins of the world and had risen again. The Christians were scattered throughout Judea and Samaria and Galilee and even as far away as Damascus. Always, they continued to preach the message of salvation offered by Christ Jesus.

Men and women were being converted everywhere: in cities, towns and country areas. But perhaps the most thrilling conversion was that of Saul.

Some of the Christians simply could not believe that their greatest persecutor was now their friend–a fellow believer in the Lord Jesus Christ. But when they saw for themselves the difference in this one who so recently had persecuted them, they knew that God had indeed changed his life. Saul was completely turned about. Instead of hating the Son of God, he now went everywhere preaching about Him. He no longer hated the Christian believers; he loved them. He was converted.

1. PETER, A JEW, HAS A VISION
Acts 10:1-16; 11:1-10

Meanwhile, many miles from Damascus, the Apostle Peter was also preaching about Jesus. God was using him in an unusual way. He healed some who were sick, raised a dead woman to life and led many to turn away from sin to serve the Lord Jesus. But even as Peter taught the wonderful truths of Christ to others, God taught Peter many new truths–truths which were hard for Peter to understand.

(*Teacher:* Locate all places on map, page 16.)

Peter was staying at the seaside near Joppa in the home of a man named Simon. Simon was a tanner, who prepared leather which was used to make sandals, ropes, belts and many useful things. Tanners, however, were not allowed to live in the city because of the smell that came from the kind of work they did. In fact, the Jews considered a tanner to be unclean because he had to kill animals and work with their hides. This they believed to be against the teachings of their religion.

Even though Peter had strong convictions about the necessity of keeping the Jewish laws, he stayed in the home of Simon. He also felt that Jews were the only ones who should be converted.

One day at noon, Peter went up to the flat roof of the house. He was hungry–but he wanted to pray.

Show Illustration #5

As he prayed, Peter saw in a vision a large sheet being let down from Heaven. Inside the sheet were many different kinds of four-legged animals, wild beasts, creeping things and birds. Then Peter heard a voice say, "Get up, Peter! Kill and eat!"

Peter was puzzled, for it was against Jewish law to eat the kinds of animals which were in the sheet. Peter answered, "Oh no, Lord, for I have never eaten anything that is common or unclean."

The voice said, "What God has made clean, you should not call common or unclean."

After the voice spoke three times, the sheet went back into Heaven. Peter was confused. What was he supposed to do? What was God teaching him?

– 21 –

2. PETER HAS GENTILE VISITORS
Acts 10:17-22; 11:11

Right then three visitors arrived downstairs. "Is this the house of Simon, the tanner?" they asked. "Yes, it is," they were told.

At that exact moment the Spirit of God said to Peter, "Three men have come to see you. Go down to meet them and go with them. Do not doubt about it, for I Myself have sent them."

Show Illustration #6

Peter hurried down to meet the waiting men. "I am the one you are looking for," he said. "Why have you come?"

They explained, "We have come from Caesarea, (about 50 kilometers away). We were sent by Cornelius, a Roman captain (in charge of 100 men). He is a good man who worships God. However, he is not a Jew. He is a Gentile." (As such, he was considered unclean by the Jews.)

The men told Peter also, "An angel of God commanded Cornelius: 'Send for Peter and listen to his message.' "

3. PETER GOES TO THE HOUSE OF CORNELIUS, A GENTILE
Acts 10:23-35; 11:12-14

As Peter listened he knew that God wanted him to go with the men to Cornelius in Caesarea. But it was too late in the day to begin the journey. So Peter invited the men to stay for the night. The next morning they went on their way, taking along some of the believers of Joppa.

Show Illustration #7

When they arrived in Caesarea they found Cornelius eagerly waiting for them. But he was not alone. He had called in all his relatives and close friends to hear what Peter would say.

Now Peter was beginning to understand why God had sent the vision of unclean animals. God was teaching him that he was not to preach to Jews only, as he had been doing. He was to reach men and women everywhere–both Jews and Gentiles. Cornelius was a Gentile. According to Jewish law a Jew was not to enter the house of a Gentile. Peter knew now, however, that God considered all people equal. There was no difference between the Jew and the Gentile.

So Peter began to speak to Cornelius and his friends. "You know it is against the law for a Jew to come into the house of anyone of another nation," he said. "But God has shown me that I should not call anyone common or unclean. So I came to you as soon as possible. Now tell me why you sent for me."

Cornelius answered: "Four days ago, as I was praying at about three o'clock in the afternoon, a man in shining clothes said to me, 'Cornelius, your prayer is heard. Your gifts are remembered by God.' Then I was told to send for you. You have done well to come so soon. Now we are all in the presence of God to learn everything that the Lord has told you to tell us."

"I am certain now that God does not look at one person above another," Peter began. "But in every nation, those who believe in Him are accepted by Him." Then Peter told about the Lord Jesus, how He went about doing good, healing the sick and casting out demons.

4. PETER PREACHES THE GOSPEL TO CORNELIUS
Acts 10:36-48; 11:15-18

Show Illustration #8

Peter explained, "The Lord Jesus was put to death on the cross and has risen again from the dead. He has sent us to preach the good news of salvation everywhere so that all may have opportunity to believe on Him and have forgiveness of sin."

Then, while Peter was speaking, a wonderful thing happened. The Holy Spirit came upon all those who were in the room. The Jews who were with Peter were amazed. The Holy Spirit came upon the Gentiles exactly as He had come upon the Jewish believers!

There was no doubt about it–God was eager to save men and women and children of all races. Peter preached and Cornelius and all his family were converted. Having placed their trust in Christ Jesus the Lord they were baptized.

From that moment on it was clear that Jesus Christ had given His life for Gentiles as well as Jews, and that God would save them just as He saved the Jews who believed in Christ the Lord.

Perhaps you have been thinking that *you* do not need to be converted. You have been living a good life and you believe your goodness will get you to Heaven. Cornelius was a good man who worshiped God. But he had never trusted in Christ. The money he gave to the poor and his prayers to God did not prepare him for Heaven. He had to believe in the Lord Jesus Christ. He had to be converted. So, too, you need to be converted if you are to be in right relationship with God–a relationship which will assure you of spending eternity with Him in Heaven.

It makes no difference what color your skin is God loves you. No matter where you live, how old or how young you are, regardless of whether you are rich or poor, good or bad, God loves you. And He wants to change your life as He changed the lives of Saul and Cornelius. Remember, there is only one way to be in right relationship to God and be certain of going to Heaven: you must be converted.

Lesson 3
A WOMAN AND A JAILER ARE CONVERTED

Scripture to be studied: Acts 16:6-40

The *aim* of the lesson: To show that many were converted because of Paul's witness.

What your students should *know*: God wants believers to tell the Gospel to others.

What your students should *feel*: A desire to please God and a desire to reach the lost.

What your students should *do*: Tell someone about the Lord Jesus Christ this week.

Lesson outline (for the teacher's and students' notebooks):
1. Lydia and her family are converted (Acts 16:6-15).
2. A demon-possessed girl is healed (Acts 16:16-21).
3. Paul and Silas are thrown into prison (Acts 16:22-26).
4. The jailer and his family believe in Christ (Acts 16:27-40).

The verse to be memorized:

Except ye be converted, and become as little children, ye shall not enter into the kingdom of Heaven. (Matthew 18:3)

> **NOTE TO THE TEACHER**
>
> Conversion is a tremendous experience in a person's life. It is a complete turning about, with these results: (1) The one who was a sinner now has forgiveness of sin; (2) He has a right relationship to God through Christ; (3) He has fellowship with God the Father, God the Son and God the Holy Spirit; (4) He has assurance of eternal life in Heaven with God, instead of being destined for eternal separation from God; (5) Instead of only an old sin nature, he has a new nature; he is a new creation in Christ Jesus.
>
> Perhaps there is in your class a "Saul"—one who seems impossible. God can change that person and use him to take the Word of God to a "Lydia," a "jailer," and many others who will turn to the Lord and be converted.
>
> God can do miracles today, just as He did in Paul's day. Do you believe this? Will you continue to be His messenger to reach the unconverted? Will you teach those who *have* been converted, helping them to grow in the things of God? Encourage them also to be faithful witnesses for Him.

THE LESSON

Saul, about whose conversion we read in Acts 9, had another name, Paul. Perhaps both names were used in his home. Saul was his Jewish name; Paul his Greek name. After Acts 13, when he began his ministry among the Gentiles, he used his Greek name. So the Saul who is spoken of in Acts 9 and the Paul of Acts 16 are the same man.

Missionaries Paul, Silas, Timothy and Luke were planning to go to Bithynia to preach the Gospel. But one day the Holy Spirit spoke to Paul and told him to go instead to Macedonia. Paul did not argue. He obeyed God and sailed across the Aegean Sea to Macedonia, located in what was then known as Asia (now known as Europe). (*Teacher:* Depending upon the ability of your students, you may want to point out that Luke who wrote the third Gospel also wrote the book of Acts. See Luke 1:3 and Acts 1:1. Before Acts 16:10, Luke writes the events as having happened to others. In Acts 16:10, however, he continues, "And after he (Paul) had seen the vision, immediately *we* endeavored to go into Macedonia, assuredly gathering that the Lord had called *us* for to preach the gospel unto them." So from now on, Luke is with the missionary party, though he does not mention his own name.)

1. LYDIA AND HER FAMILY ARE CONVERTED
Acts 16:6-15

The Holy Spirit led these missionaries to a large Macedonian city–Philippi–an idolatrous city ruled by the Romans. Paul and the others were strangers. They knew no one in this place. They would have started their witness by preaching in a synagogue, but there was no synagogue. If only ten Jewish men lived in the city, there could have been a synagogue. But apparently most of the people in Philippi were pagans and worshiped false gods.

Where there was no synagogue, the Jewish people usually met together by the side of a river where they said prayers. So Paul and the others searched for worshipers at the riverside.

Show Illustration #9

On the Sabbath Day (Saturday, the Jewish day of worship) they found those who had gathered to pray. When the missionaries looked at the group, they saw no men–only women. How did Paul feel about this? In Paul's early life, as a strict Pharisee, he repeated every day, "O God, I thank You that I am neither Gentile, nor slave, nor woman." But Paul no longer felt this way. He knew now that all were to hear the Gospel, whether they were Jews or Gentiles, slaves or free men, men or women.

Paul began to speak to this group of women. As he spoke, Lydia, a businesswoman who sold beautiful purple cloth, listened thoughtfully. She often prayed to God and worshiped Him. But she did not know Him personally through Jesus Christ. As Paul spoke, the Lord opened her heart and she believed and received the Gospel message. She was converted–she and her whole family. Then they were baptized. Lydia wanted to know more about the Lord Jesus, and she wanted others to know Him. So she begged the missionaries, "Please stay in my home while you are in Philippi." This they agreed to do.

2. A DEMON-POSSESSED GIRL IS HEALED
Acts 16:16-21

Show Illustration #10

Day after day Paul and the others went to the riverside meeting place to speak and to pray. Each day they were followed by a slave girl who had an evil spirit within her. This girl, through the power of the demon, made her living by telling people what would happen to them in the future. She also made a lot of money for the evil men who owned her. As she followed the missionaries she shouted, "These men are servants of the Most High God! They show us the way of salvation."

What she said was the truth. But Paul was distressed to see the power of the evil spirit in her. He knew that he, as a Christian, had power within him that was far greater than the

– 23 –

power in the slave girl. So, turning to the girl, Paul said to the spirit that was in her: "I command you in the name of Jesus Christ to come out of her!"

Immediately the spirit left her. From that moment on the girl was changed. No longer did she tell about the future. This made her owners angry. Never again could they make money from her fortune-telling. They were so furious that they grabbed Paul and Silas and dragged them into the marketplace where civil trials were held. To the judges, they shouted, "These Jewish men are causing a lot of trouble in our city. They teach our people things which are against the Roman laws!"

3. PAUL AND SILAS ARE THROWN INTO PRISON
Acts 16:22-26

Their accusations stirred up the crowds which had gathered. The mob turned against Paul and Silas. The rulers, in great anger, tore the clothes from the two men and ordered them beaten with whips. Again and again their bare backs were slashed painfully. Then they were sentenced to prison. The jailer was ordered to guard them carefully.

I shall keep them securely, he thought to himself. *They will never break out of this prison. I shall throw them into the inner dungeon and lock their feet tightly in stocks.*

This is exactly what he did. He did not care that their backs were sore and bleeding. Carefully he bolted all the gates.

Paul and Silas were not alone in the cell. There were other prisoners nearby. Do you think Paul and Silas grumbled and complained about their problems? No! Instead, they did something which amazed the other prisoners. In fact, what they did was unheard of in a dungeon.

Show Illustration #11

Paul and Silas began to pray and sing. Imagine that! No matter how much their bleeding backs hurt them, they sang praises and worshiped God in the darkness of the prison.

At night the jailer did not hear the singing. He was asleep. But the other prisoners listened to their songs of praise to God.

Suddenly, at midnight, there was a great earthquake. The foundations of the prison were shaken. The doors flung open. The chains and the stocks fell off. The prisoners were free to escape from prison.

4. THE JAILER AND HIS FAMILY BELIEVE IN CHRIST
Acts 16:27-40

The terrified jailer knew he would be put to death if a prisoner escaped. Quickly he drew his sword–preferring to kill himself rather than to be slain by the authorities.

Paul shouted, "Do not hurt yourself! We are all here!"

The jailer could hardly believe it. "Bring me a light!" he ordered, and with it rushed into the dungeon. There stood the prisoners, free from their stocks and chains.

Show Illustration #12

The jailer fell trembling before Paul and Silas. Finally he led the two men out of the dirty dungeon. "What must I do to be saved?" he asked.

They answered, "Believe on the Lord Jesus Christ and you will be saved–you and your household."

The jailer gathered his family and servants. They listened to Paul who told them the message of God: they could be saved from their sin by turning to the Saviour, Christ Jesus the Lord.

The jailer was sorry for his sin and for the cruel way he had treated Paul and Silas. He took them aside and washed their wounded backs. Then he and his family and servants, having been converted, were baptized. He and all in his house were full of joy because of their new faith in Christ.

In the morning the judges sent the police officers to the jailer, saying, "Let those men go." They had probably been frightened because of the earthquake during the night.

The keeper of the prison was glad to tell Paul the good news. "The judges say you are to go free," he said.

But Paul was not satisfied. He answered, "They have beaten us in public without giving us a fair trial, even though we are Roman citizens. They threw us into prison. But now they want us to leave secretly. No, indeed! Let them come themselves and lead us out."

The police officers hurried back to the judges and told what Paul had said. When the judges heard that these two men were Roman citizens, they were afraid. If the Emperor heard that two Roman citizens had been punished without a trial, the judges would be in serious trouble.

So the judges themselves came to the prison and begged Paul and Silas to leave. Then they led the freed men from the prison.

But before the apostles left the city, they made one last visit to the home of Lydia. There they encouraged the new believers, said good-bye and left to preach the Gospel in other cities of Europe.

Do you, like Paul and Silas, want people to be converted? Are you willing to be used of God? Will you go wherever He wants you to go, even if it means being mistreated? There will be glory for those who are faithful in suffering for the cause of Christ. (See Romans 8:17-18; 1 Peter 4:13-16.) Will you tell others the Word of God which says, "Except you are converted, and become as little children, you will not enter into the kingdom of Heaven" (Matthew 18:3)?

Lesson 4
CONVERSION

NOTE TO THE TEACHER

Conversion is possible only by the power of God. The Holy Spirit of God works upon the human heart, mind and will in such a way that the person's life is completely changed. He is turned about.

When the Apostle Paul wrote to the converts in Thessalonica, he said they had "turned to God from idols to serve the living and true God" (1 Thessalonians 1:9). This should be the experience of every truly converted person. We turn *to* God; we turn *from* idols (sin); we serve God. And our service for the Lord is done wherever we are. For Cornelius it probably meant remaining in the army. Lydia doubtless kept on selling her purple cloth. The jailer may have continued his jail-keeping. But each was at once concerned for the conversion of families and friends–a concern which we believe they never lost.

Paul started a new career after his conversion. He became a Gospel preacher and a foreign missionary. Some converts are called by God for this holy purpose. But *all* converts–children, young people, soldiers, all people everywhere–should be faithfully serving the Lord every day no matter where they are or what they are doing. (See Colossians 3:22-24; Ephesians 2:10.) Are you that kind of convert?

Scripture to be studied: Acts 8:5-24

The *aim* of the lesson: To show that true conversion is through the work of the Holy Spirit in a person's life.

What your students should *know*: A person is not converted until he places his trust in Christ.

What your students should *feel*: A desire to receive Christ as Saviour.

What your students should *do*:
Unsaved: Believe that Jesus is the Son of God, admit to their sinfulness and receive Christ as Saviour.
Saved: Share their conversion experience with others.

Lesson outline (for the teacher's and students' notebooks):
1. Philip preaches Christ in Samaria (Acts 8:5-12).
2. Simon desires Philip's power (Acts 8:13-17).
3. Simon tries to buy Philip's power (Acts 8:18-24).
4. True conversion affects every part of a person's life (2 Corinthians 5:17).

THE LESSON

In our last three lessons we talked of one woman and three men who were converted. Who were they? (Encourage discussion.) Saul, Cornelius, the Philippian jailer and Lydia were truly converted.

What does conversion mean? (It means "to turn about completely.") Saul, a Jew, did just that. He turned to God and new life in Christ, and turned away from sin and the old life. Cornelius was a Gentile who was a praying and giving man. But he did not know the Lord Jesus. When he learned of Him, he willingly turned to God away from his sin. So did the Philippian jailer and Lydia, the woman who sold purple cloth.

Is it possible for some to hear the good news and *pretend* to be converted? Can outsiders presume they have turned to God from sin? Listen carefully!

1. PHILIP PREACHES CHRIST IN SAMARIA
Acts 8:5-12

Show Illustration #13

A man named Simon lived in the city of Samaria. He was famous for the amazing things he could do through his magical powers. Many people listened to him and followed him, watching the strange tricks he performed. Some said, "This man must be the great power of God." But he was not a miracle-worker from God–he was a deceiver. So skillful was Simon that for a long time the people of the city gave him much attention. One day, however, someone with greater power than that of Simon came to Samaria. That someone was Philip.

Philip had come to these mystified Samaritans to preach about the Lord Jesus Christ. They listened carefully to him. Never had they heard such words as his. They also saw things they had never seen before: sick people were healed; lame men were enabled to walk; demon-possessed men and women were set free from tormenting evil spirits. As the people listened to Philip and saw these wonderful miracles, many turned to Jesus Christ as Saviour. They let others know about their conversion by being baptized.

2. SIMON DESIRES PHILIP'S POWER
Acts 8:13-17

Show Illustration #14

Simon listened to the powerful words of life and saw the amazing miracles. He thought, *Philip does things I have never been able to do. I wonder how he does it. He has a power that is greater than mine.* The more Simon thought about it, the more he wanted to be like Philip.

At last he went to Philip saying that he too believed in Jesus and wanted to be baptized.

Of course no one knew what was in Simon's heart–no one but God.

Meanwhile, Peter and John heard about the good meetings that were being held in Samaria and came to help Philip. They were glad when they saw how many people had turned to Jesus Christ. Peter and John prayed for these people that the same power of the Holy Spirit which had come upon the disciples in Jerusalem might come upon these in Samaria. Then, laying their hands on the new believers, Peter and John prayed for them–and the Holy Spirit came also upon the Samaritans.

3. SIMON TRIES TO BUY PHILIP'S POWER
Acts 8:18-24

Simon, who had been watching, was more amazed than ever. If he could have the same power as these disciples, he would indeed be a popular man.

– 25 –

Show Illustration #15

Secretly he spoke to the apostles. "I will give you money for this power that you possess. Will you sell it to me so that anyone on whom I place my hands may receive the Holy Spirit?" (He wanted the people to turn back to following him.)

Peter answered, "How dare you think that the gift of God can be bought with money! Your heart is not honest in the sight of God. Turn from this great wickedness and pray that the Lord will forgive you. You are bound by your own sin."

Simon answered, "Pray for me so nothing will happen to me." He did not say anything about wanting to be forgiven. He just wanted to escape punishment. And this is the last time he is mentioned in the Bible.

Simon was a pretender. He had not been truly converted.

4. TRUE CONVERSION AFFECTS EVERY PART OF A PERSON'S LIFE
2 Corinthians 5:17

There are many today who call themselves Christians. But they are not genuinely convinced by the Holy Spirit that they are the children of God. (See Romans 8:16.) There are four truths to be remembered. So you can always have them with you, will you please write the following facts in your notebook?

To be truly converted:

1. A person must *believe* that Jesus is the Son of God who died on the cross to save him from sin. (See John 3:16; 1 Corinthians 15:3-4.)
2. A person must *admit* that he himself is a sinner who needs a Saviour. (See Romans 3:23.) A person cannot turn to God from his sin if he does not recognize that he is a sinner.
3. He must *want* to be saved.
4. Each one must make a decision. To be converted, a person must receive Christ into his heart and life. (See John 1:12; Revelation 3:20.) A person must say: I now come to Him and receive Him as my Saviour from sin.

Conversion is a tremendous blessing. It affects every part of our being–our mind, our conscience, our heart and our will.

It is possible, however, to experience one, two or three of the four truths we have just listed in our notebooks without really being converted. One might say, "I believe that Jesus Christ is the Son of God." Yet that person may never have been converted. Another might quickly admit he is a sinner and knows it without a doubt. But that does not convert him. It is possible to turn from sin without turning to God.

Many want to be saved. But that does not convert them.

To be converted one must be able to say honestly from the heart: "I *believe* Jesus is the Son of God. I *admit* that I am a sinner and need a Saviour. I *want* to be saved. I *now receive* Christ as my Saviour."

Saul could honestly say: "I *believe*, I *admit*, I *want* and I *now receive* Him." Cornelius also could make the same statements. So could the Philippian jailer and Lydia. But what about Simon? Poor Simon! He could say, "I see that Jesus is the Son of God." He could also say, "I ought to come to Him. I admit I need Him." But did he say honestly, from the heart, "I now come to Him and receive Him as my Saviour"? No, he simply wanted the great power the disciples had. If only Simon had said in his heart, "I now receive Jesus as my Saviour."

Today, the important question is: Have *you* been converted?

Conversion is the work of God in the heart. It is the result of turning by faith to God from sin. It is being delivered from the power of darkness into the kingdom of God's Son. (See Colossians 1:13.) It is turning to freedom from bondage. It is turning to heavenly things from earthly things. It is turning to eternal life from eternal death.

If you have been converted, you can share the blessed news with others. Do not keep it a secret. Let others see and know that because you have turned to serve the living God, you have turned from your sin. Explain to them that with childlike faith (as our memory verse reminds us) they can receive the Lord Jesus as Saviour and have assurance of eternal life. Then they too will be able to say:

1. I *believe* that Jesus is the Son of God who died on the cross to save me from sin.
2. I *admit* that I am a sinner and need a Saviour.
3. I *want* to be saved.
4. I *now receive* the Lord Jesus as my Saviour.

One of the evidences that a person is truly converted is that he shares his faith with others. Will you be this kind of Christian this very week? With whom will you share the good news?

www.ingramcontent.com/pod-product-compliance
Lightning Source LLC
Chambersburg PA
CBHW060803090426
42736CB00002B/139